W9-BLC-130

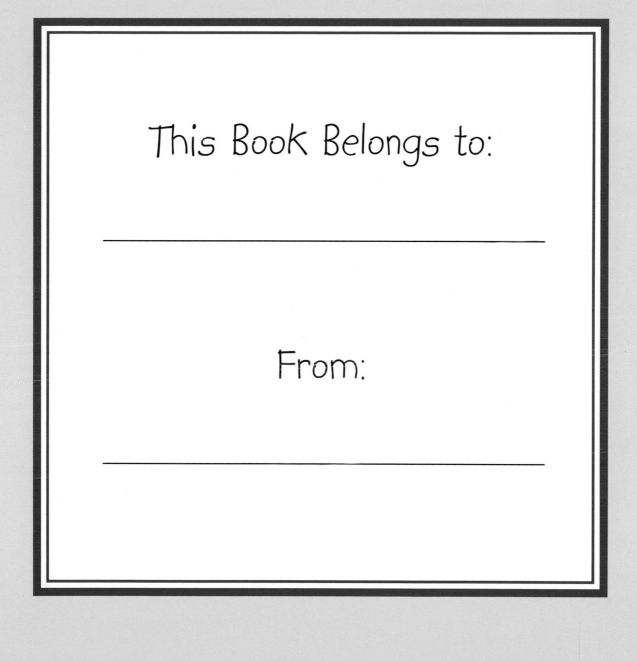

This Book Belongs to:

_____

From:

_____

The Story of Jesus

ISBN 0-8249-5545-5

Published by Ideals Children's Books
An imprint of Ideals Publications
A Guideposts Company
535 Metroplex Drive, Suite 250
Nashville, Tennessee 37211
www.idealsbooks.com

Copyright © 2006 by Ideals Publications

All rights reserved. No part of this publication may be reproduced or transmitted in any form or by any means, electronic or mechanical, including photocopy, recording, or any information storage and retrieval system, without permission in writing from the publisher.

Color separations by Precision Color Graphics, Franklin, Wisconsin

Printed and bound in Italy by LEGO

Library of Congress CIP data on file

Designed by Jenny Eber Hancock
Cover design by Georgina Childlow-Rucker

10 9 8 7 6 5 4 3 2 1

Jesus promised
that He would
be with us forever.
When we
pray,
we ask Jesus
to help us.

The Story of Jesus

By Patricia A. Pingry • Illustrated by Rebecca Thornburgh

ideals children's books.
Nashville, Tennessee

Jesus is the
son of
God.
He loves us
very much.

We celebrate Jesus'

birthday

at Christmas.

On Easter,

we remember

that Jesus gave

His life

for us.

We read
in the Bible
about Jesus
and His
twelve
disciples.

Jesus was

very

kind.

He said,

"Love one another

as I love you."

One day,
some children
came up to Jesus.
His friends said,
"Go away.
Jesus is tired."

But Jesus said,
"Let the little children
come to me.
All people
should have the
faith
of a little child."

Jesus performed

many

miracles.

He made

sick people well.

One day,
Jesus was preaching.
The people got
very hungry.
One little boy had
five rolls
and
two fish
for his lunch.

The boy gave it
to Jesus to share.
Jesus fed
5,000
people with the
boy's lunch.

We love

Jesus

because

He first

loved us.